MW01153743

Explorers & Exploration

The Travels of Henry Hudson

By Joanne Mattern
Illustrated by Patrick O'Brien

Raintree Steck-Vaughn Publishers
A Harcourt Company

Austin · New York
www.steck-vaughn.com

Published by Raintree Steck-Vaughn Publishers,
an imprint of Steck-Vaughn Company

Library of Congress Cataloging-in-Publication Data
Mattern, Joanne
    Henry Hudson / by Joanne Mattern
       p. cm—(Explorers and exploration)
    Includes index.
    Summary: A biography of the English explorer and sea captain who explored three North American waterways later named for him—the Hudson River, Hudson Bay, and Hudson Strait.
    ISBN 0-7398-1483-4
       1. Hudson, Henry, d. 1611—Juvenile literature. 2. Explorers—America—Biography—Juvenile literature. 3. Explorers—England—Biography—Juvenile literature. 4. America—Discovery and exploration—English—Juvenile literature. [1. Hudson, Henry, d. 1611. 2. Explorers. 3. America—Discovery and exploration—English] I. Title. II. Series.

E129.H8 M37 2000
970.01'7—dc21   99-055476

Printed in the United States of America
10 9 8 7 6 5 4 3 2 1 LB 03 02 01 00

Produced by By George Productions, Inc.

Illustration Acknowledgments
p. 4, 22–23, 27, 28, 30, 34, 36–37, New York Public Library Picture Collection; p. 38, Tate Gallery, London/Art Resources, New York; p. 25, Corbis; p. 41, John Blazejewski; p. 42, Frank Sloan
All other artwork is by Patrick O'Brien

Contents

THE HALF MOON AT YONKERS.

THE DUTCH ON MANHATTAN

HIGH upon the walls of the go
ernor's room in the capitol of t
Knickerbockers, among the gra
chief magistrates of state and cit
hangs a small, dingy canvas, in
tarnished frame of antique workma
ship. Upon it was depicted, mo
than two hundred years ago, perha
by the Vandyke-taught pencil of V.
der Helst, a broad-ruffled, short-ha
ed portrait, with an expansive, inte
lectual forehead, and a countenan
full of the dignity and courtly bea
ing of an honorable gentleman
the time of the First King James
England. They are the features
a navigator, whose history is like

HENRY HUDSON.

Hudson's Early Life

The 1500s and 1600s are called the Age of Exploration. During this time brave sea captains and their crews sailed all over the world. These men were searching for new lands and new treasures.

One of the greatest of these explorers was Henry Hudson. As a young boy growing up in London, England, Henry was thrilled by the stories of adventure he heard on the city's docks.

Experts don't know much about Henry Hudson's early life. He was born in England around 1570. Historians think he was the grandson of an important London person, also named Henry Hudson. The elder Hudson helped start the Muscovy Company. The Muscovy Company traded English wool for Russian furs and gold. Young Henry Hudson may have worked in his grandfather's offices.

Henry Hudson was born in England toward the end of the 16th century.

5

Experts are not sure when Henry Hudson first went to sea. He probably served as a cabin boy on several voyages. Cabin boys helped the captain and the crew with many jobs.

When cabin boys reached the age of 16, they became apprentices. At this time they learned to read sea charts and forecast the weather. They also had to care for the sails and other parts of the ship, and navigate, or sail. Boys were apprentices for seven years. So Henry was at least 23 years old before he could call himself a sailor. We don't know what ships he sailed on or where he traveled when he was young. Most likely he went on journeys to the Mediterranean Sea, the North Sea, and Africa. He might even have sailed to North America.

Food on board ship was mostly stews and hardtack. The food often was invaded by pests.

Life on board ship was difficult. The crew ate a heavy biscuit, which had little flavor. It was called hardtack. Stews made of meat, carrots, onions, and barley were also common. Water was stored in large barrels, but it often became dirty. Food often spoiled or got worms in it.

Sailors slept in thin, hanging beds called hammocks. They swayed back and forth with the motion of the ship. This could be very unpleasant if the seas were rough!

By 1607 Hudson had married a woman named Katherine and had three sons—Oliver, Richard, and John. John would go with his father on all four of his voyages.

Hudson's fame as a sailor had grown over the years. By 1607 the Muscovy Company liked Hudson's work. They agreed to make Hudson captain of one of their ships on a dangerous journey to the Far East. Hudson would look for a new trade route to China and India.

Countries in the Far East had spices and jewels. Europeans wanted to take these things home.

The First Voyage

During the Age of Exploration, many sea captains were looking for a shorter route to the Far East. Asian countries such as India and China had spices, jewels, and other things that were wanted in Europe. Trading with the East became a big business. But the only way to get to Asia was to sail around Africa. This trip took months. Sailors knew that they needed to find a shorter route to Asia. Then they could make more trips back and forth and sell more goods.

Many explorers tried to find a northern route to Asia by sailing north of Europe and into the Arctic Ocean. But ice and bad weather meant the ships could not get through. Still, people kept trying. Their ideas sound foolish today. But many people in Hudson's time knew that the sun shines almost all day and night during summers at the North Pole. They believed the sun could melt the ice and make a clear path to Asia. This path was known as the Northeast Passage.

Hudson believed in the Northeast Passage. He talked to the leaders of the Muscovy Company about sailing across the North Pole to Asia. They agreed to pay for his voyage and gave him a ship called the *Hopewell*. At last Henry Hudson was captain of a ship! An excited Hudson found a crew and got the *Hopewell* ready to sail. The ship left London on April 19, 1607.

For the first six weeks of the journey, the weather was fine. The sun shone warmly, and winds pushed the *Hopewell* north at a good pace. But this good luck did not last. The sun went away and the weather became colder. Soon it was so cold the sails froze. A thick fog rolled in, making it hard to see where the ship was going. The ship rocked wildly in the fierce winds. The sailors feared the sails would rip!

Hudson and his men sailed on. They traveled around the eastern coast of Greenland and reached warmer weather near some islands named Spitsbergen, north of Norway. From the ship the men saw many animals—seals, walruses, and geese.

The water was filled with hundreds of gray whales. There were so many whales that they rubbed against the ship. Hudson named the spot Whales Bay. But just a few days later, a thick wall of ice blocked the *Hopewell's* path.

Henry Hudson discovered Whales Bay, which was filled with gray whales. This discovery was the beginning of the English whaling trade.

By now food was running out on the *Hopewell*. The ice was thick and the weather was freezing. Hudson knew that there was no way to sail to the North Pole. In August he turned back to England.

Hudson did not find a Northeast Passage. But his discovery of whales led to the beginning of the English whaling industry. Whales were hunted and killed for their meat, oil, and bones. Whale blubber was especially good because it could be made into soap and oil for lamps. The whaling industry brought a great deal of money to the Muscovy Company. Henry Hudson's first voyage was said to be a great success.

A Second Try

Henry Hudson still wanted to find a Northeast Passage. The Muscovy Company was so happy with his first trip that they agreed to pay for another.

During the winter of 1607–1608, Hudson studied maps and planned the next trip. He decided not to sail straight to the North Pole. Instead, he would go east of the Pole, toward the coast of Russia.

Many of the men who had sailed with Hudson on his first voyage did not want to join him again. They remembered the bad conditions and terrible ice. So Hudson hired a mostly new crew of 14 men. He also signed up his son John as the cabin boy.

One of the men Hudson hired was Robert Juet. Juet was about 50 years old and was a good sailor. Hudson made Juet his first mate. That meant Juet was second in command after Hudson. It was his job to make sure the crew followed the rules.

THREE OF HENRY HUDSON'S VOYAGES

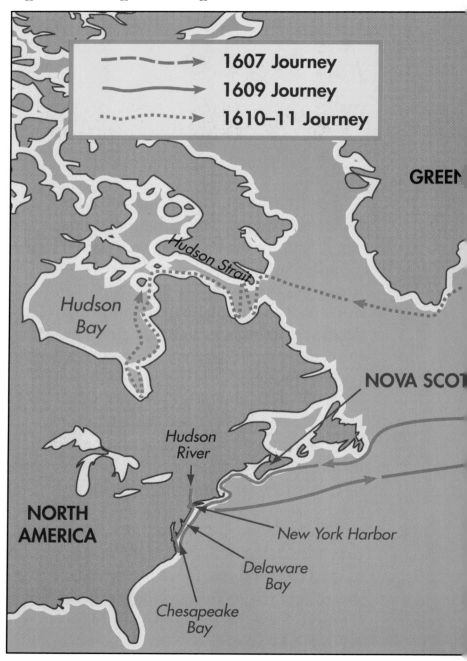

1607 Journey
1609 Journey
1610–11 Journey

GREEN

Hudson Strait

Hudson Bay

NOVA SCO

Hudson River

NORTH AMERICA

New York Harbor

Delaware Bay

Chesapeake Bay

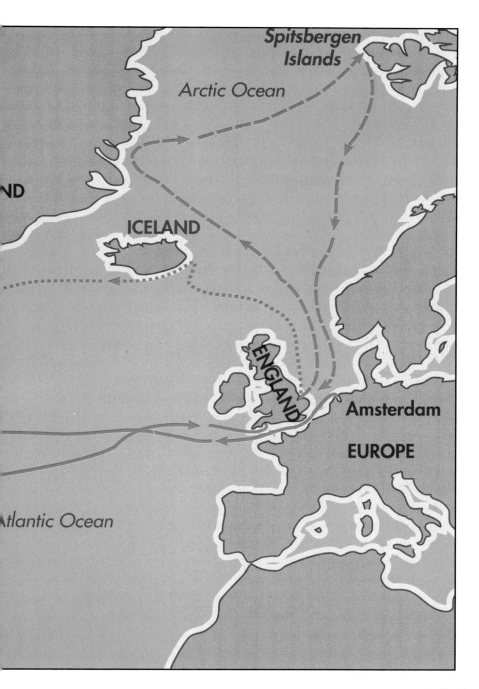

Spitsbergen
Islands

Arctic Ocean

ICELAND

ENGLAND

Amsterdam

EUROPE

Atlantic Ocean

The *Hopewell* left London on April 22, 1608. Things went well at first. But in early June a frightening thing happened. Hudson was steering through a field of ice floes. Floes are large pieces of ice. He noticed that the ice was beginning to pack closer and closer. He looked behind him and saw the same thing happening. If the ice became too tightly packed, the ship would be trapped. The men would either freeze or starve to death. Hudson was finally able to steer the ship out of danger. But his crew was scared and unhappy.

By the end of June, the ship had reached the Russian islands of Novaya Zemlya in the Arctic Circle. On July 2 a lookout saw a large river. Maybe this was the Northeast Passage! Hudson sent out a few men in a rowboat to explore. They returned with bad news. The river was too shallow for a large ship. This was not the Northeast Passage.

Ice floes pressed against Hudson's ship, creating danger.

Soon the weather turned cold and stormy. Hudson knew he could not sail east any more. He turned the ship to the west. His crew thought they were returning to England. But Hudson decided to sail across the Atlantic Ocean to North America. Maybe he would find a passage to the Far East there.

When Hudson's crew realized what was happening, they became angry. Led by Robert Juet, they threatened to take over the ship. This is known as a mutiny. Unless Hudson turned back to England, a mutiny might take place. Hudson had to agree to what they asked.

The sailors worried that Hudson might report their threat of mutiny. As the ship's captain, he could have his men arrested or even put to death. So they forced Hudson to sign a statement. It said that he was turning back of his own free will, not because of threats from his men. Hudson's second voyage had failed.

Henry Hudson was a good sailor who often disagreed with members of his crew.

The Greatest Voyage

When Hudson reported the results of his second voyage to the Muscovy Company, they were not happy. In fact they told Hudson they no longer wanted him to work for them.

Hudson was upset but still wanted to find a Northeast Passage. He went to Holland to talk with the Dutch East India Company. It was a business that traded goods between Europe and the Far East.

People at the Dutch East India Company had heard about Hudson and wanted to meet with him. But they would not make any promises about a voyage.

While Hudson waited for an answer from the Dutch, King Henry IV of France sent a man to talk to him about sailing for France. When the members of the Dutch East India Company heard about the meeting, they sent for Hudson. They told Hudson they wanted him to sail for them, not for France. They gave Hudson a small, 60-foot (18-m)-long ship called the *Half Moon*. The members also made Hudson sign a statement saying he must only look for a passage east of the North Pole. He was not to try any other routes.

Hudson wanted to hire an English crew, but the Dutch East India Company insisted that half the crew be Dutch. Hudson was able to get Robert Juet as first mate again. He could be difficult, but he was a good seaman. Hudson also brought his son John on board as a sailor. On April 6, 1609, the *Half Moon* sailed out of Amsterdam, Holland.

Hudson's third voyage did not get off to a good start. The weather was cold and stormy. The Dutch and English crew did not get along with one another. By mid-May, the ship had only reached Norway.

Hudson gathered his crew together and told them he had a great idea. Before he left Holland, he had received a letter from his old friend Captain John Smith. Captain Smith had founded the English settlement of Jamestown, Virginia. He told Hudson that the Native Americans spoke of a great sea that led to the Pacific Ocean. Hudson was sure that this was a Northwest Passage—a shorter route to the Far East!

Hudson and his crew sailed to what is now North America.

Hudson read the letter to his crew. Even though the Dutch East India Company had asked him to sail east, he wanted to sail west toward America. The sailors were so tired of the cold, difficult conditions that they agreed. Hudson turned the ship around and headed for America.

The *Half Moon* crossed the Atlantic Ocean in less than a month. The sailors reached the coast of what is now Canada. Then they headed south, searching for the Northwest Passage. Along the way groups of Penobscot Indians came on board the ship to trade goods. Robert Juet said the Indians "showed us great friendship." But he and the other sailors did not trust these people.

The Indians learned not to trust the sailors. In July the sailors attacked an Indian village on what is now the Penobscot River. The sailors drove the Indians away from their houses and stole all of their goods. Hudson quickly sailed away, fearing that the Indians would attack the ship.

Hudson sailed down the North American coast for more than a month. He reached what is now Cape Hatteras, North Carolina. Then he turned back and began exploring every body of water, searching for the Northwest Passage.

A view of the Hudson River today

Early on the morning of September 2, the *Half Moon* sailed into what is now New York Harbor. Hudson saw the mouth of a large river and decided to explore it. Today that river bears his name—the Hudson River.

The sailors passed many wonderful sights as they sailed up the river. They saw cliffs and giant oak trees. Hudson called the land "the finest for cultivation that I ever in my life set foot upon."

As Hudson sailed farther north, the river became very narrow. By late September, Hudson

knew that this river was not the Northwest Passage. The *Half Moon* turned around and headed back toward the Atlantic Ocean.

During their trip on the river, Hudson and his crew had many friendly meetings with American Indians. Some invited Hudson to great feasts. Hudson also held a feast on board the ship for Delaware and Mohican leaders. But there was also conflict. In one fight, a sailor, John Coleman, was killed. Later sailors kidnapped two Indians.

American Indians await the arrival of Henry Hudson's ship at New York Harbor.

**Hudson and his men met many American Indians
during their time on what is now the Hudson River.**

ᒧᒧ

By the beginning of October, the *Half Moon* had almost reached the mouth of the river. The ship stopped to trade with Indians, who came on board. Conflict suddenly broke out. Two Indians were killed. Others jumped overboard. Hudson and his crew sailed farther down the river.

Items used by the American Indians Hudson met on his 1609 voyage—bows and arrows, canoes, and clothing.

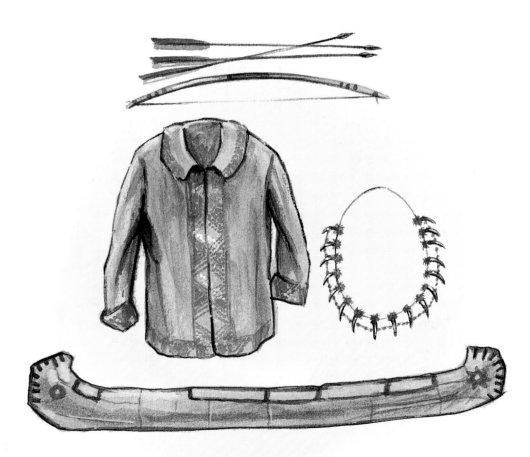

The next day fighting broke out again. Several Indians were killed in the battle. Hudson was nervous about attacks on the *Half Moon*. He sailed as fast as he could to the mouth of the river and into the Atlantic Ocean.

Hudson wanted to keep exploring North America until he found the Northwest Passage. But his crew wanted to go home. The ship had little food and supplies. Hudson finally agreed.

With the ship low on supplies, Hudson's crew was eager to return to Europe.

The Final Voyage

The *Half Moon* docked at Dartmouth, England, on November 7, 1609. Hudson sent a report of the trip to the Dutch East India Company and asked for money for another voyage. But the company wanted more details about the trip Hudson had just finished before they would pay for another one.

While Hudson was in England, King James I heard about his trip. The king was angry that Hudson, an Englishman, had worked for another country. He had Hudson brought back to London and kept him under arrest in his own home. This is known as house arrest. Hudson sat at home and waited to hear if the king would try him.

Many people in England were angry when they heard about Hudson's arrest. A group of men went to King James. They convinced him to let Hudson out so he could sail under the English flag. These men even raised the money to pay for a ship and a crew.

By the spring of 1610, Hudson had a new ship, the *Discovery*. His crew was made up of many sailors who had worked with him before, including Robert Juet. There was also a new sailor named Henry Greene. Greene had a bad temper and often got into fights. But he had been a good friend to Hudson while the captain was under house arrest. Hudson's son John would also be making the voyage with his father.

Hudson and his crew left London on April 17, 1610, and set out across the Atlantic. Soon Henry Greene began causing trouble and fighting with the other men. Robert Juet began spreading tales that Hudson had told Greene to spy on the other sailors. Hudson did his best to calm the crew and headed west toward North America.

By June 15 the *Discovery* reached the coast of what is now Quebec, Canada. About two weeks later, the ship sailed into what is now called the Hudson Strait.

The sailors were frightened by the rough tides, ice, and fog. They begged Hudson to turn back. Instead, the captain sailed on for more than 400 miles (643 km). On August 2 the *Discovery* sailed into a large body of calm water. For another month the ship sailed south. Everyone hoped they had found the passage to the Far East.

The crew saw that land cut off their journey. The sailors were in a bay, an enclosed body of water. Today this large bay is known as Hudson Bay. Hudson and his crew realized that this could not be a passage to the Pacific Ocean.

The weather grew colder, and the bay filled with ice. An angry Juet told the other sailors the ship was lost. He said that Hudson would let them all die. Hudson was angry when he heard this and put Juet on trial. Juet was given a lower rank. Hudson also punished other sailors who had spoken against him. These actions caused more bad feelings between the crew and Hudson.

By November the *Discovery* was trapped in the ice of Hudson Bay. There were few supplies on the ship. And there were no fish or animals for the men to hunt. They couldn't even find any plants or fruit to eat. Many men became sick, and a few died. Some fought with each other and with Hudson. The fact that Hudson treated some of his men better than others only made things worse.

It was early June before the ice melted enough to free the ship. Hudson headed west, still hoping to find a passage to the Far East. But most of his sailors didn't like their captain. They just wanted to go home.

Hudson's ship, the *Discovery*

Henry Greene, Robert Juet, and a few other sailors began to plot a mutiny. They spread stories that Hudson was keeping food for himself and his friends. Many sailors believed that if they didn't get rid of Hudson, they would all die.

On the morning of June 22, 1611, three men grabbed Hudson as he was leaving his rooms. They tied him up and put him into a rowboat. Hudson's son John and other loyal crew members were also forced into the boat. Then the boat was set adrift without any supplies. Henry Hudson and his companions were never seen again.

Ice floes often trapped ships in Hudson Bay. This is a ship similar to Hudson's _Discovery_.

Henry Greene named himself captain of the *Discovery* and headed back to England. The journey was hard, because none of the men knew how to read Hudson's charts or navigate. By the time the *Discovery* reached England in the fall of 1611, all the leaders of the mutiny were dead. Henry Greene died in a fight with Eskimos shortly after the mutiny. Robert Juet starved to death during the trip across the Atlantic.

Only eight sailors returned to London. By the time a trial took place in 1618, four had died. The court tried the last four sailors for murder, not mutiny. But murder could not be proved. The court freed the sailors.

What happened to Henry Hudson? No one is sure. Most historians think he and his companions died, either from the cold or from starvation. Others believe that Hudson and his men made it to shore and were taken in by a group of Cree Indians. Some legends say that a group of Inuit found a boat full of dead white men. Others say that another group of American Indians captured the men and made them slaves.

Henry Hudson, his son John, and a few others were left at sea. They were never seen again.

Other legends say that Henry Hudson's ghost still haunts the waters that bear his name. Stories of a ghost ship sailing up the Hudson River were once common there.

No matter what happened to him, Hudson is remembered today as one of history's greatest explorers. His name lives on in the northeastern parts of North America—places such as the Hudson River, Hudson Bay, and Hudson Strait. And his voyages helped Europeans learn more about the world and led to new settlements in North America.

Today Henry Hudson's name is still well known in North America.

A photo of the Hudson River, north of
New York City

Other Events of
the 17th Century
(1601 – 1700)

During the century that Henry Hudson was exploring North America, events were happening in other parts of the world. Some of these were:

1608   French explorer Samuel Champlain founds the settlement of New France in what is now Canada.

1632   Italian scientist Galileo Galilei supports the idea that the sun, and not Earth, is the center of the solar system.

1642–1649   King Charles I of England and the country's parliament fight for leadership. The conflict is known as the English Civil War.

1643   The Taj Mahal, a building surrounded by gardens, is completed in India. Emperor Shah Jahan had it built in memory of his wife.

1644   Ch'ing Dynasty is established in China.

1652   Foundation of Cape Colony by the Dutch.

1659   French found trading station on Senegal coast of Africa.

Time Line

1570?	Henry Hudson is born.
April 1607	Hudson sets sail as captain of the *Hopewell*.
June 1607	Hudson discovers hundreds of gray whales near the Spitsbergen Islands and names the spot Whales Bay.
August 1607	Trapped by ice in the Arctic, Hudson is forced to return to England.
April 1608	Hudson and the *Hopewell* leave London on a second voyage to explore the northern coast of Russia, searching for the Northeast Passage.
July 1608	Bad weather and sailing conditions force Hudson to abandon his search. He heads for North America, but his crew threatens a mutiny and Hudson returns to England.
January 1609	Hudson is hired by the Dutch East India Company and given the ship the *Half Moon*.

April 1609	The *Half Moon* sails from Amsterdam to North America in search of a Northwest Passage.
May–October 1609	Hudson explores the northeastern coast of North America and sails up the river now known as the Hudson River.
November 1609	The *Half Moon* arrives in England.
1610	King James I of England puts Hudson under house arrest for working for a Dutch company.
April 1610	Aboard the *Discovery*, Hudson explores the coast of Canada.
1611	The *Discovery* is trapped in ice in Hudson Bay. Hudson and his crew face hard conditions, including starvation and disease.
June 1611	Hudson's crew mutinies and sets Hudson, his son John, and other loyal crew members adrift in a small boat. They are never seen again.
Fall 1611	The eight members of Hudson's crew who made it back to London are tried for mutiny.

Glossary

apprentice (uh-PREN-tis) Someone who learns a trade or craft by working with a person who is skilled in that field

Arctic (ARK-tik) The frozen area around the North Pole

bay A part of the ocean that is partly enclosed by land

blubber (BLUB-er) The fat of whales and other sea mammals, used to make soap or lamp oil

cabin boy (KAB-in boy) A young boy who does chores on a ship

Far East The countries of East Asia, including China, Japan, Korea, and Mongolia; sometimes the countries of Southeast Asia and the islands of Malaysia are included

first mate The highest-ranking officer on a ship after the captain

floe (flo) A large mass of floating ice

hardtack A heavy, flavorless biscuit often eaten on long sea voyages

historian (his-TORE-ee-uhn) A person who studies the past

house arrest (hous uh-REST) Being held as a prisoner in your own home

legend (LEDGE-und) A story passed down through history, often based on fact but not necessarily true

mutiny (MUTE-uh-nee) A rebellion in which sailors refuse to obey the captain and take control of the ship

navigate (NAV-uh-gate) To travel using maps and instruments to find your way

Northeast Passage (north-eest PASS-ij) A sea route connecting the Atlantic and Pacific oceans along the northern coasts of Europe and Asia

Northwest Passage (north-west PASS-ij) A sea route connecting the Atlantic and Pacific oceans along the northern coast of North America

strait (strayt) A narrow strip of water that connects two larger bodies of water

whaling (WALE-ing) Hunting and killing whales for their meat, oil, and bones

Index